Did you hear that Jeffrey Dahmer broke out of prison?

He was last seen in an A-1 Steak Sauce truck heading for Waco, Texas.

———————

Are English teachers half-assed?

No, they're semi-coloned.

———————

What's a politician's definition of safe sex?

No reporters around.

———————

What's the difference between a wife and the IRS?

Once a wife catches you cheating she *stops* screwing you.

———————

Who was more messed up than Oedipus?

Adam . . . he was Eve's mother.

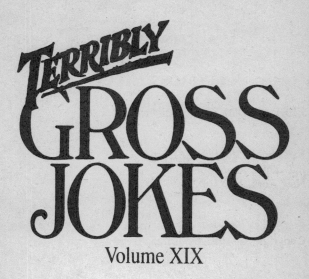

TERRIBLY GROSS JOKES

Volume XIX

by Julius Alvin

ZEBRA BOOKS
KENSINGTON PUBLISHING CORP.

ZEBRA BOOKS are published by

Kensington Publishing Corp.
850 Third Avenue
New York, NY 10022

First Printing: March, 1995

Printed in the United States of America

Table of Contents

One

Men & Women

Raunchy realities

Did you hear about the dork who finally got a steady job at a drugstore?

He stood outside and made people sick.

_____

How can you tell if a woman is tough?

She rolls her own tampons.

_____

Why shouldn't a woman hold in a fart?

Her tampon might pop out.

———

Why do women have periods?

Because they deserve them.

———

What do you do if your daddy's got a hard-on?

Call Mom!

———

It was at a Sunday service at a Methodist church that a man and woman went up to the front of the church together. The woman lit a candle, and, taking the man's hand, spoke to the congregation.

"We're lighting this candle in honor of our five beautiful years together, and for the gratitude we feel for all the love and good cheer all of you have given us and our little girl."

As the couple began moving back to their seats, a voice from the back of the church sounded, "But when are you getting married?"

———————————

Under the old apple tree,
'Twas up her dress I could see
A little brown spot,
She called it her twat,
But it looked like her asshole to me.

———————

Why do stuck-up bitches do it doggie-style?

Because they hate to see anyone else having fun.

———————

Why do Canadians do it doggie-style?

So they can both watch the hockey game.

———————

What's the quickest way to ruin a man's ego?

"Is it in yet?"

———————

What's the quickest way to empty a men's bathroom?

"Nice dick!"

———————

Sue: What's that in your frying pan? It looks like a dick.
Miggy: It is. I've tasted that bastard's dick raw so many times, now I want to taste it cooked.

———————

Fortune teller: Mrs. Kinloch, I have some bad news. Your husband is going to die a violent death, very soon.

Mrs. Kinloch: Oh. Will I be acquitted?

———————

There once was a fucker named Young
Who said he was very well hung.
When they asked him to prove it,
He said, "Nothing to it!"
And he pulled up his dick to his tongue.

———————

Old Humphry went to see a doctor. His problem was unique and quite painful. He had a swollen, raw, twisted dick. The doctor examined him and found nothing that might cause such a problem. Then he began to probe Humphry's medical history.

"Do you have a normal sex life?"

"Yes."

"Do you urinate normally?"

"Well, no. I always have trouble when I take a piss. I can't really describe it."

"Can you show me how you urinate?"

"Okay, doc, if you say so." Humphry pulled out his dick and some urine dribbled from the tip. "Look at this," he said, watching it ooze like a damp rag. After a few moments of intermittent dripping, he grasped his dick with both hands and wrung it out.

"I think I know a treatment," said the doctor.

"What's that?"

"Amputate both arms," the doctor replied.

Two

Heterosexuals

Raunchy jokes on
straight men and women

What did the CEO say when asked
whether he talks to his wife during sex?

"Sure, if she calls."

_____

Did you hear about the deaf gynecologist?

He learned how to read lips.

_____

Did you hear about the horny Indian?

He jumped into a canoe, took three strokes, and shot across the lake.

———————

Did you hear about the hunter who found out that his wife was having an affair with his best friend?

He rushed home and shot his dog.

———————

SIGN AT A FUNERAL HOME: Our staff will stuff your stiff.
SIGN AT A WHOREHOUSE: Our stuff will stiff your staff.

———————

Chester and Ethel, both eighty years old, decided after 55 years of marriage that they should get a divorce. Six months later, Chester called up Ethel to brag. "Ethel, I've got me a beautiful, blonde, twenty-one year-old girlfriend."

Ethel was not one to be outdone. "Chester," she said, "I've got a stunningly handsome twenty-one year-old Adonis. And I'll tell you what: twenty-one goes into eighty more than eighty goes into twenty-one.

———————

What's the difference between a toilet and a dumb blonde?

A toilet doesn't follow you around after you're done using it.

———————

How can you tell a dumb blonde is having her period?

She's only wearing one sock.

———————

What do pantyhose and Saddam Hussein have in common?

They both irritate Bush.

———————

What's the difference between ooh and aah?

About three inches.

———————

If you ever have a piece of ass, what should you do?

Turn it over—there's pussy on the other side.

———————

Two surveyors, a man and a woman, were working in the field together. The man was at one end of the survey area, and signaled to the woman that he needed a hammer. He did this by pointing at his eye, then at his knee, then hammering on the ground. The woman signaled back. She pointed at her eye, then grabbed her left tit, then pointed at her pussy. The man, still wanting a hammer, signaled again, and the woman signaled back. After several more exchanges, the man still hadn't gotten a hammer. He was furious. Finally, he stomped all the way over to the woman and said, "Goddammit, I need a hammer!"

The woman answered, "I told you, I left it in the box!"

————

What do you call a male concubine?

Concubone.

———————

A guy walked into a gift shop and asked the lady behind the counter, "Do you keep stationery?"

She answered, "Yes, right up to the last moment. But then my toes curl up, and I turn into an animal!"

———————

A lady walked into a hardware store and asked the guy behind the counter how she could fix her broken door lock.

"You wanna screw for the lock?" he asked.

"No, but I'll blow you for a toaster."

———————

A railroad conductor worked on the run between Chicago and Cleveland. One day he had a layover in his home town, so he called his wife.

"Hey, baby, I'll be home tonight."

"Should I get undressed?" she asked.

"Hell no," said the conductor. "I just got time to come and go, not to chew the fat."

———————

Have you heard of Eva Braun's diary?

It's called Mein Kunt.

———————

How do you find an old man in the dark?

It's not hard.

———————

Why was everyone so happy at the donkey roast?

They all got a piece of ass.

———————

Why is sex like Jell-O?

There's always room for more.

———————

A couple stayed at the hotel where they had had their honeymoon twenty years earlier. "Tell me," said the woman, "What were you thinking twenty years ago?"

"I was thinking, 'Baby, I'm gonna fuck your brains out.'"

"What are you thinking now?"

"It worked!"

———————

Why is Madonna like a tampon?

They're both stuck up cunts.

How does a rock 'n' roll babe know she had a good time on a date?

She throws her panties against the wall and they stick.

What's grosser than getting pubic hair stuck in your teeth?

Waking up after an orgy with a lump in your throat and a string hanging out of your mouth.

Did you hear about the retired tampon manufacturer?

He liked to keep a finger in his business.

———————

Missy: Do you make friends quickly?
Buffy: Yes, but with strangers it takes a
little longer.

———————

What's a car accident?

Getting impregnated in the back seat.

———————

How did the bimbo prove she wasn't on the pill?

She stood up.

———————

How do you graduate from Hooker U?

"Some-a Cum Louder."

———————

What does a woman with a yeast infection do?

Scratch and sniff.

———————

What's the difference between poverty and a Jewish woman?

Poverty sucks.

———————

What's the difference between a young hooker and an old hooker?

Vaseline and Poly-Grip.

———————

Grayson, an older woman, ran flying into the hotel and up to the counter shouting, "I have to see Jock Williams."

The clerk told her, "I'm sorry, Ma'am, I don't have a Jock Williams here."

"Yes you do—I saw him come in!"

"Lady, we don't want any trouble. He's in room 832."

Grayson went up to room 832 and rapped on the door, which was answered by a beautiful woman. Through clenched teeth, Grayson said "I want to see Jock Williams."

"He's not here."

Grayson burst into the room and saw Jock Williams laying naked on the bed. She picked him up and threw him out the window. "What'd you do that for?" asked the girl.

"At eighty-five, if he can fuck, he can fly."

Why is incest like watching TV?

The whole family does it together.

———————

Why don't Frenchmen eat flies?

They can't get their little legs apart.

———————

How do you know Bambi's mother was a prostitute?

She fucked for bucks.

———————

Walking down Canal Street, looking for a whore.

God damn son of a bitch, couldn't find a whore.

Finally found a whore, she was tall and thin.

God damn son of a bitch, couldn't get it in.

Finally got it in, twist it all about.

God damn son of a bitch, couldn't get it out.

Finally got it out, it was red and sore.

The moral of this story is, never fuck a whore.

———————

What's the best way to eat a frog?

Put its little legs over its ears.

———————

Why doesn't Santa Claus have any children?

Because he only comes once a year, and always down the chimney.

———————

A bum showed up at a whorehouse one day and said to the clerk, "Listen, I only got two bucks. What can you do for me?" The clerk told him to go up to the third floor, second door on the left.

The guy went up to the third floor, second door on the left, and there on the bed was a beautiful blonde woman with huge tits. He shouted "YAHOO!" and flung himself on top of her. After he had been bouncing passionately on her for several minutes, he noticed a gooey white substance coming out of her ears, her nose, her mouth, and her eyes.

He was overcome by disgust. He scrambled off the bed, ran down the stairs and out the front door, screaming all the way. The clerk saw him fly past, and called into the back room, "Hey, Leon, the dead one's full again!"

Three

Homosexuals

Raunchy jokes
about gays and lesbians

Did you hear about the dumb blonde lesbian?

She picked up men.

What's the difference between a dike and a lesbian?

A dike kick-starts her dildo.

What do you call lesbian twins?

Lick-alikes.

———————

How did Martina Navratilova become a champion?

She licked the pants off her opponents.

———————

Why is Martina Navratilova such a good tennis player?

Because she can go lickety-split.

———————

Why isn't Martina Navratilova allowed to play tennis in the Netherlands?

She wants to stick her finger in every dike.

———————

Why is heaven going broke?

Because Michaelangelo is up there blowing all the prophets.

———————

Why is a queer like a grocery store?

They both take meat deliveries in the back.

———————

A gay man went to a doctor and said, "Doc, I got a problem with my ass." The doctor took an x-ray and found a vibrator stuck up the man's ass.

"This will have to be surgically removed," the doctor told him.

"No, don't take it out," said the man. "Just put in new batteries."

———————

Did you hear about the gay burglar?

He couldn't blow the safe, so he went down on the elevator.

———————

What's a gay man's favorite Chinese food?

Cream of Sum Yung Gai.

———————

What's an organ grinder?

A queer with a broken tooth.

———————

Why did the gay man's car insurance get canceled?

He got rear-ended too often.

———————

How does a lesbian hold her liquor?

By the hair.

———————

First Lesbo: Let's do lunch.
Second Lesbo: Who eats who?

———————

What's the difference between a lesbian and a postage stamp?

None. They both get sticky when you lick 'em.

———————

When Rock Hudson arrived at the Pearly Gates, St. Peter refused to let him in because Rock supposedly had eaten a parakeet. Rock denied that he had ever eaten such a bird. But after a little more questioning, he finally admitted that he did eat a cockatoo.

———————

What do you call two queers named Bob?

Oral Roberts.

———————

What do you call a Chinese fag?

Chew man chew.

———————

What do you call an Irish fag?

Gay lick.

———————

What do lesbians get before they get married?

A liquor license.

———————

Why did the gay man decide not to sell his car?

He found out he could blow the horn.

———————

What does a gay man call seafood?

A sailor.

———————

Did you hear about the straight football player who unwittingly walked into a gay bar?

At first he was a Straight Blocker. After a few drinks, he was an Offensive Lineman. Soon after that, he was a Tight End. Before the night was over, he had become a Split End and a fabulous Wide Receiver!

Four

Celebrities

Amy Fisher, Jeffrey Dahmer, and
other stars

What's the quickest way to commit suicide?

Tell Amy Fisher you just fucked Joey.

———————

How do you save Amy Fisher from drowning?

Throw her an anchor.

———————

Why did Joey Buttafuoco start dating Amy?

He was looking for a playmate for his inner child.

———————

Where did Amy Fisher buy her vibrator?

Twats 'R' Us.

———————

What does Amy Fisher do when she climaxes?

She drops her pistol.

———————

How do you tell when Amy Fisher is having her period?

You can't—she's got PMS every day.

———————

Why did Joey Buttafuoco want Amy Fisher to go to church?

She was good at playing his organ.

———————

What did the ad for Jeffrey Dahmer's apartment say?

Roommate included, some assembly required.

———————

What did Jeffrey Dahmer say to his late-arriving guest?

"Sorry you're late. Everyone's eaten."

————————

What's Milwaukee's favorite beer?

Dahmer Beer. It has lots of body but no head.

————————

Why did Jeffrey Dahmer keep a head in his refrigerator?

Because a mind is a terrible thing to waste.

————————

Did you hear that Jeffrey Dahmer broke out of prison?

He was last seen in an A-1 Steak Sauce truck heading for Waco, Texas.

———————

Why wouldn't anyone play cards with Jeffrey Dahmer?

He might come up with a good hand.

———————

What did Jeffrey Dahmer say to the cops who arrested him?

"Have a heart."

———————

What do Jeffrey Dahmer and Saddam Hussein have in common?

They both have a fetish for collecting arms.

———————

What's the difference between Jeffrey Dahmer and Charles Manson?

Charles Manson didn't like finger sandwiches.

———————

How did Jeffrey Dahmer describe the men in his life?

"They taste just like chicken."

———————

What's Jeffrey Dahmer's favorite movie?

Eating Raoul.

Have you heard about the new TV show about David Koresh?

It's called, "Married to Children."

Why is Shannen Doherty's new perfume called "Come to Me?"

Because, she says, "It smells like cum to me!"

Why is Madonna such a cunt?

Because you are what you eat.

Five

Pros & Hobbyists

Gross jokes about work and play

What's the difference between tennis players and golfers?

Tennis players have fuzzy balls.

What's the difference between mechanics and businessmen?

Mechanics have better tools.

What's the difference between Dutchmen and Swedes?

Swedes have meatballs.

——————————

Why do policemen have bigger balls than firemen?

They sell more tickets.

——————————

Why do lawyers have more laundry than other people?

They do it in their briefs.

——————————

What does an Irish feminist say on St. Patrick's Day?

Erin go bragh-less!

———————

Have you heard about the sadistic urologist?

He's called Dr. Kutznutzoff.

———————

How did the impotent soldier finally make his mistress happy?

He got a discharge.

———————

What's something that even the finest tailor in the world cannot do?

Sew a button on a fart.

———————

A gunslinger went into a saloon and ordered a beer. Standing next to him at the bar was none other than Doc Holliday himself. The gunslinger introduced himself, bragged about his speed, and shot a cufflink off the piano player as a demonstration of his skill.

"Kid," said Doc Holliday, "if you go down to the blacksmith and shave a hair off that gun, you'll be able to shoot a lot quicker."

The gunslinger had his gun shortened, came back in the saloon, and shot the other cufflink off the piano player. This time he was indeed able to shoot quicker.

"Kid," said Doc Holliday, "you might want to go out back and roll that gun in the lard."

"Will that make me faster?"

"Nope, but it'll make it a lot easier on you when Wyatt Earp gets done playing that piano."

———————

What do you call a farmer with a pig under one arm and a sheep under the other?

Bisexual.

———————

Did you hear about the dumb blonde who went to Hollywood to get into the movies?

She fucked the studio custodian.

———————

What do you call an African American hooker?

Rent-a Kunt-ay.

———————

How does a surrogate mother advertise?

"Womb for rent."

———————

Are English teachers half-assed?

No, they're semi-coloned.

———————

What's damp and yellow and covered with hair?

A drunk professor in a urinal.

———————

How can you tell that a biologist is a good date?

He's a fungi.

———————

Some anthropologists were studying the Native Americans in Quebec. They were preparing to travel with the tribe, and so they dashed off a note to their suppliers with a request for two punts and a canoe. A week later they received a card from their supplier saying, "The girls are on the way, but what the hell is a panoe?"

———————

Why are meteorologists such great lovers?

They have warm fronts.

———————

Why are telephone operators such great lovers?

They have no hangups.

———————

Why are photographers such great lovers?

They're better developed.

————————

Why are stamp collectors such great lovers?

They stick to it.

————————

Why are fishermen such great lovers?

They have long, stiff rods.

————————

Why are fishermen such careful lovers?

They do it with flies.

————————

Why are pilots such great lovers?

They do it full throttle.

———————

Why are painters such great lovers?

They know all the strokes.

———————

Why are pizzamakers such great lovers?

They call ten inches small.

———————

Why are marines such great lovers?

They don't pull out until ordered.

———————

Why are scientists such great lovers?

They oscillate.

———————

Why are pianists such lousy lovers?

They do it with their fingers.

———————

Why are beer drinkers such lousy lovers?

They use foam.

———————

Why are proctologists such lousy lovers?

They do it bass ackwards.

———————

Why are publishers such lousy lovers?

They only do it periodically.

———————

Do old auto racers ever die?

No, but they're hard on tires.

———————

Do old bowlers ever die?

No, they just don't score as much.

———————

Do old milkmen ever die?

No, they just curdle.

———————

Pregnant woman: Doctor, what should I do if I start having the baby before I get to the hospital?

Doctor: Just get in the same position you were in when you conceived, and let nature take its course.

Pregnant woman: You mean hanging off a tree branch thirty feet over Central Park?

———————

One day, Bernie was out fishing, and having no luck at all. After three hours he was ready to go home. He glanced down the end of the pier, and he saw a man pulling in fish after fish. Bernie watched for a few moments, and saw the man catch four more fish. He had to know how he did it.

He walked down to the end of the pier and said to the man, "Excuse me, but I couldn't help noticing that you're catching an awful lot of fish. Can I ask, where do you buy your bait?"

The man looked up and said, "Oh, I don't have to buy bait. I do circumcisions for a living."

Six

Gross Baby Jokes

Things not to tell a pregnant person

What's blue and sits in the corner?

A baby in a plastic bag.

———————

What's green and sits in the corner?

The same thing a week later.

———————

What's red and sits in the corner?

A baby with a razor blade.

———————

What's red and swings back and forth?

A baby on a meathook.

What's red and white and hangs from a tree?

A baby hit by a snowblower.

What's pink and red and waves wildly?

A baby in a blender.

What's brown and lumpy and drools?

A baby in a pot of stew.

What's brown and bubbly and knocks on the window?

A baby in a microwave.

———————

What's worse than finding a hundred dead babies in a garbage can?

Finding one dead baby in a hundred garbage cans.

———————

What's worse than a hundred dead babies in a garbage can?

Ninety-nine dead babies in a garbage can with a live one on the bottom eating its way out.

———————

What's the difference between a truckload of dead babies and a truckload of bowling balls?

You can't unload bowling balls with a pitchfork.

———————

What do you call a dead baby?

Dinner.

———————

What do you call a baby that got run over by a truck?

Flatty.

———————

What do you call a baby that fell down a flight of stairs?

Lumpy.

———————

What can you use a dead baby for?

A flyswatter.

————————

What can you use five dead babies for?

A footstool.

————————

How do you fit a hundred babies in a Volkswagen?

La Machine.

————————

How do you get them out?

With a straw.

————————

How do you make five babies shingle a roof?

Slice them thin.

———————

Why does a newborn baby have a soft spot on its head?

So you can carry it with one finger.

———————

Why should you give alcohol to a crying baby?

So you don't have to stick its head in the oven.

———————

Ed: Hey, there's a fly in here.
Joe: Quick! Get me a dead baby!

Seven

No Arms or Legs

In classic bad taste

What do you call a guy with no arms or legs floating in the pool?

Bob.

———————

What do you call a guy with no arms or legs hanging on the wall?

Art.

———————

What do you call a guy with no arms or legs on the ledge?

Cliff.

———————

What do you call a guy with no arms or legs on the porch?

Matt.

———————

What do you call a guy with no arms or legs who's not feeling well?

Chuck.

———————

What do you call a guy with no arms or legs flying over a lake?

Skip.

———————

What do you call a guy with no arms or legs on the stove?

Bern.

_____

What do you call a guy with no arms or legs in a restaurant?

Tip.

_____

What do you call a guy with no arms or legs who's a florist?

Bud.

_____

What do you call a guy with no arms or legs who got hit by a steamroller?

Miles.

———————

What do you call a guy with no arms or legs who's underweight?

Graham.

———————

What do you call a guy with no arms or legs stuck in a toilet?

John.

———————

What do you call a guy with no arms or legs under your car?

Jack

_____

What do you call a guy with no arms or legs on the barbeque?

Frank.

_____

What do you call a guy with no arms or legs lying on the ground?

Herb.

_____

What do you call a guy with no arms or legs flying over the fence?

Homer.

———————

What do you call a guy with no arms or legs who works for the president?

Vito.

———————

What do you call a guy with no arms or legs wearing a raincoat?

Flash.

———————

What do you call a guy with no arms or legs in the ditch?

Phil.

———————

What do you call a guy with no arms or legs and six girlfriends?

Dick.

———————

What do you call a guy with no arms or legs and a five-inch tongue?

Felix.

———————

What do you call a cowboy with no arms
or legs?

Buck.

_____

What do you call a guy with no arms or
legs and no clothes on?

Seymour.

_____

What do you call a guy with no arms or
legs in your mailbox?

Bill.

_____

What do you call a guy with no arms or legs who's buried in a mud-slide?

Clay.

———————

What do you call a guy with no arms or legs and a cold?

Fleming.

———————

What do you call a guy with no arms or legs and a two-inch dick?

Tad.

———————

What do you call a guy with no arms or legs and an airbrush painting on him?

Van.

_____

What do you call a dead guy with no arms or legs?

Barry.

_____

What do you call a cremated guy with no arms or legs?

Ernie.

_____

What do you call a girl with no arms or legs?

Carrie.

———————

What do you call a girl with no arms and a wooden leg?

Peg.

———————

What do you call a girl with no arms or legs every four weeks?

Flo.

———————

What do you call a girl with no arms or legs and four wheels?

Dolly.

———————

What do you call a girl with no arms or legs hanging from the ceiling?

Tiffany.

———————

What do you call a girl with no arms or legs from Mexico?

Can-Swallow.

———————

What do you call a girl with no arms or legs who works for an English freight company?

Lori.

_____

What do you call a girl with no arms or legs who hates the English?

Erin.

_____

What do you call a girl with no arms or legs on the barbeque?

Patty.

_____

What do you call a girl with no arms or legs lying facedown?

Fannie.

———————

What do you call a girl with no arms or legs sitting on a slice of bread?

Marge.

———————

What do you call a girl with no arms or legs on the side of a building?

Ivy.

———————

What do you call a girl with no arms or legs and six boyfriends?

Hedy.

What do you call a girl with no arms or legs surrounded by six truckers?

Dinah.

What do you call a girl with no arms or legs who's a lawyer?

Sue.

What do you call a girl with no arms or legs and an ego?

Mimi.

———————

What do you call a girl with no arms or legs lying on the beach?

Sandy.

———————

What do you call a girl with no arms or legs and only one eye?

Iris.

———————

What do you call a girl with no arms or legs who tells fortunes?

Crystal.

———————

What do you call a guy with no arms or legs sitting in the closet?

Dusty.

———————

What do you call a girl with no arms or legs sitting in the closet?

Lint-sey.

———————

What do you call a guy with legs cut off at the knees?

Neil.

———————

What do you call a guy with one arm, no legs, and no girlfriend?

Hand Solo.

———————

What do you call a promiscuous girl with no arms or legs?

Lay-a.

———————

What do you call a woman with one leg?

Eileen.

———————

What do you call a Chinese woman with one leg?

Irene.

———————

What do you call a Chinese hooker?

Cha-Ching.

———————

What do you call a woman with AIDS?

Diane.

———————

What do you call a man who likes oral sex?

Oedipus.

———————

What do you call a man who charges for anal sex?

Horace.

———————

What do you call a man who likes AC/DC?

Turner.

———————

What do you call a guy with a permanent hard-on?

Woody.

———————

What do you call a guy with no arms or legs and diarrhea?

Shit outta luck!

Eight

Politicians & Lawyers

Gross jokes about professional snakes

Why is Jimmy Hoffa no longer in the Teamsters?

He was dismembered.

———

What's the "Pat Buchanan Bucket" at Kentucky Fried Chicken?

A bucket full of right wings and assholes.

———

What was the longest six years of Pat Buchanan's life?

The third grade.

_____

What's a politician's definition of safe sex?

No reporters around.

_____

Why did Michael Griffin shoot the abortion doctor?

To impress Jodie Foster.

_____

Why can't you sue a hooker?

Because a blowjob doesn't qualify as an oral contract.

_____

What do you call an attorney with an I.Q. of 50?

Your Honor.

_____

What has 18 legs and four tits?

The Supreme Court.

_____

Why don't sluts ever vote?

They don't care who gets in.

_____

Why is Joan Rivers like Chicago?

They're both chronically plagued by winds.

———————

What do Marion Barry and Marilyn Quayle have in common?

They both blow a little dope.

———————

Name a feminist revolutionary.

Leon Twatsky.

———————

What do Velveta Cheese and the Princess Di have in common?

They're both easy to spread and fit for a king.

———————

How can you tell Nixon is an idiot?

He had to do it sixteen times before he got it down Pat.

———————

Reporter: Governor, do you believe in capital punishment?
Governor: Yes, but I don't believe women should be hung like men.

———————

One day, in pre-war Germany, a school-teacher was praising Hitler and describing the great benefits that Hitler had bestowed on the German people. "He is like a father to us," the teacher told his class. "Is there anything that you children would ask your father to do for you?"

"Yes," said a Jewish boy. "Make me an orphan."

Nine

Cannibals & Corpses

An appetizing selection

What factor determines whether cannibals hang out in bars or not?

It depends if they're on a diet.

What's a cannibal's favorite pick-up line?

"Your oven or mine?"

What's a cannibal's idea of a relaxing evening at home?

Having a couple people over for dinner, then renting a movie.

———————

What's a cannibal's idea of the perfect evening out?

Meeting for drinks, going to a show, then having a late-night bite.

———————

What did the cannibal at the restaurant say?

"Waiter, there's no finger in my soup!"

———————

How does a cannibal describe the flavor of chicken?

"It tastes just like human."

———————

What's a cannibal's favorite meal?

Ribs of the opposite sex.

———————

How does a cannibal compliment the chef?

"He was finger-lickin' good."

———————

What's a cannibal's favorite side dish?

Human beans and rice.

———————

What's a cannibal's biggest fear?

Having to become a vegetarian.

———————

Where is the best place to put a headless body?

In the chili.

———————

What are the benefits of headlessness?

You don't have to wear a hat, you can ignore those "Hair Club" ads, and you get instant weight loss.

———————

What can a person with no head do for a living?

Not much.

———————

How do decapitated people smell?

Badly.

———————

What's a decapitated person's favorite food?

Head cheese.

———————

What is a headless body good for?

A speed bump.

———————

Why did knights returning from battle use to give severed heads to their children?

They wanted them to get ahead in life.

———————

A lawyer died in a small town. The funeral director took delivery of the remains, and asked the family, "Would you like me to bury him, embalm him, or cremate him?"

His family answered, "Better do all three."

Ten

What's The Difference Between . . . ?

Callous comparisons

What's the difference between a lightbulb and a bowling ball?

A lightbulb gets screwed; a bowling ball only gets fingered.

What's the difference between a head-on collision and a blow-job?

In a head-on collision you can see the prick coming.

What's the difference between a basketball player and a young lover?

None. They both dribble before they shoot.

———————

What's the difference between a wife and the IRS?

Once a wife catches you cheating she *stops* screwing you.

———————

What's the difference between Baghdad and the women at the Tailhook Convention?

None. They were both assaulted by Patriot missiles.

———————

What's the difference between a chess player and a gay man?

A gay man would never sacrifice a queen.

What's the difference between Hot Lips Hoolihan and David Koresh?

None. They both had Major Burns all over them.

What's the difference between rhubarb and pussy?

Nobody eats rhubarb.

What's the difference between a hobo and a homo?

A hobo has no friends; a homo has friends up the butt.

What's the difference between a hedonist and a transsexual?

A transsexual wants to eat, drink, and be Mary.

What's the difference between kinky and perverted?

Kinky is when you fuck a sheep; perverted is when you marry it.

What's the difference between pantyhose and Brooklyn?

None. They both have a Flatbush in the middle.

———————

What's the difference between an old man and a cock?

When you hold a cock the wrinkles disappear.

———————

What's the difference between Jack Nicklaus and Liberace playing golf?

Jack Nicklaus could out-drive you but Liberace could lick you in the putz.

———————

What's the difference between foreplay and Thanksgiving?

None. You start nibbling on some leg, thigh, and breast, then you move on to the stuffing.

———————

What's the difference between a near-flush in poker and a brothel?

A near-flush has four hearts; a brothel has whore farts.

———————

What's the difference between the Pope taking a shower and a Republican?

None. They both look down on the un-employed.

———————

What's the difference between a vagina and a motel room?

In a vagina you leave your bags outside.

———————

What's the difference between a nympho-maniac and a Macintosh?

None. They're both user friendly.

———————

What's the difference between the Bermuda Triangle and a virgin?

The Bermuda Triangle swallows seamen.

———————

What's the difference between Penthouse and National Geographic?

None. They both show exotic places you'll never be in.

———————

What's the difference between a plaque and a plick?

A plaque hangs on a wall, a plick hangs on a Chinaman.

———————

What's the difference between a safety instruction and Liberace's dildo?

A safety instruction is handle with care; Liberace's dildo is a candle with hair.

———————

What's the difference between toy trains and titties?

None. They're both meant for kids but daddies like to play with them too.

———————

What's the difference between a reflex exam and a nut?

A reflex exam is a tickle-test; a nut is a test-tickle.

———————

What's the difference between a cat and a kitten?

A cat scratches and claws, but a little pussy never hurt anybody.

———————

What's the difference between a dead camel and a frigid woman?

None. They're both dry humps.

––––––––––

What's the difference between a computer and a woman?

When a woman goes down on you, its foreplay; when a computer goes down on you, you're fucked.

––––––––––

What's the difference between a cucumber and a man?

A cucumber will never ask you to swallow its seed.

––––––––––

What's the difference between a squirrel and a man?

A squirrel likes having his nuts crushed.

What's the difference between Richard Gere's boyfriend and Jay Leno's hair?

None. They both get blown daily.

What's the difference between butter and a hooker?

None. They're both spread for bread.

What's the difference between masturbation and transplantation?

With masturbation, the organ never gets rejected.

————————

What's the difference between an interpreter and someone who performs oral sex?

None. They're both cunning linguists.

————————

What's the difference between Pac Man and a whorehouse?

In Pac Man it only costs you 25¢ to get eaten three times.

————————

What's the difference between a circumcised penis and a cheapskate?

One of them leaves a tip.

———————

What's the difference between a Southern treat and an ice-cream dildo?

A Southern treat is a corn pone; an ice-cream dildo is a porn cone.

———————

What's the difference between a professional goalie and a woman?

Goalies wears more pads because their periods come every twenty minutes.

———————

What's the difference between a gay sergeant and a masturbator?

None. They both play with their privates.

What's the difference between Oedipus and an Egyptian necrophiliac?

One is a motherfucker; the other is a mummy fucker.

What's the difference between Biblical times and modern times?

In Biblical times first you commit adultery, then you get stoned.

What's the difference between a microwave and buttfucking?

A microwave won't brown your meat.

What's the difference between a comedian and a gynecologist?

A comedian sees both men and women crack up.

What's the difference between Avis Rent-a-Car and a second-rate gynecologist?

None. They're both not #1, but they're right up there.

What's the difference between a woman and a golf course?

A woman has a hole in the middle of the rough.

———————

What's the difference between Donna Rice's political preferences and her sexual preferences?

In her heart she preferred Bush but in her bush she preferred Hart.

———————

What's the difference between a lawyer and a pit-bull?

The attache case.

———————

What's the difference between jelly beans and men?

Jelly beans come in different colors.

———————

What's the difference between an egg and a screw?

You can beat an egg.

———————

What's the difference between a fox and a pig?

About a dozen beers.

Eleven

Iraq

A target of american jokes and jets

What's the difference between an Iraqi and a pair of jeans?

Jeans have only one fly.

_____

What's the difference between a hypodermic needle and an Iraqi?

None. They're both a pain in the ass.

_____

What's the difference between an Iraqi woman and a catfish?

One has whiskers and smells like a fish. The other lives in water.

———————

What's the difference between US pilots and Iraqi pilots?

US pilots break ground and fly into the wind; Iraqi pilots break wind and fly into the ground.

———————

Why can't you circumcise Iraqis?

Because there is no end to those pricks.

———————

Why don't they have sex ed in Iraq any more?

Because the camel died.

———————

Why do Iraqis wear robes?

Because a camel can hear a zipper a mile away.

———————

How do you save an Iraqi from drowning?

Take your foot off his head.

———————

Why is it so cheap to train the Iraqi Air Force pilots?

They only have to be taught to take off.

———————

How do you identify an Iraqi airliner?

There's hair under the wings.

———————

Why did the Iraqi trade his wife for an outhouse?

The hole was smaller and it didn't smell as bad.

———————

What do you call a beautiful woman in Iraq?

A tourist.

———————

What's the difference between the Jews and the Iraqis?

The Jews have it behind them.

———————

What do Hiroshima, Nagasaki, and Baghdad have in common?

Nothing, yet.

———————

How does an Iraqi commit suicide?

He smells his armpit.

———————

What's an Iraqi Mercedes?

A 1972 Chevy Vega.

———————

What's the difference between a disaster and a catastrophe?

When a planeload of Iraqis crashes, that's a disaster. When it lands safely in New York, that's a catastrophe.

Twelve

Religious Jokes

Even the clergy enjoy sex

Why did Jesus cross the road?

He was nailed to the chicken.

_____

What did Jesus say when he returned to earth and tried to do some modern dancing at a night club?

"Help! I've risen and I can't get down!"

_____

What do you get if you cross an atheist with a Jehovah's Witness?

Someone who rings your doorbell for no reason.

———————

What does a priest say to nun when he fucks her?

"Thee holy pole is in your hole, so wet your ass and save your soul."

———————

Did you hear about the gay rabbi?

He kept blowing his shofar.

———————

What's black and white and has a dirty name?

Sister Mary Elizabeth Fuckface.

———————

What's the difference between a vulture and a Jewish mother?

The vulture waits until you're dead before it eats your heart out.

———————

What's the dirtiest thing a priest ever said?

"To go together is a blessing; to come together is divine."

———————

Why is a priest like a Christmas tree?

They both have balls for decoration only.

———————

What does a Hindu say after he takes a bite of steak?

"Father, is it really you?"

———————

Who was more messed up than Oedipus?

Adam . . . he was Eve's mother.

———————

What do Catholic boys and Justice Clarence Thomas have in common?

They can fuck up, refuse to confess, and still get confirmed.

————————

What do you get when you cross an orangutang with Jerry Falwell?

An ignorant, uneducated asshole who likes bananas.

————————

What does a Jewish woman have between her legs?

Her labia menorah.

————————

What happened when King David went to Mount Olive?

Popeye beat the shit out of him.

———————

What did God do when Moses started diddling his slave girls?

He made the Eleventh Commandment: "Thou shall not show thy rod to thy staff."

———————

Why is the birth rate among Orthodox Jews falling?

The Rabbi won't let them pork.

———————

What's white and falls from the sky?

The coming of the Lord.

Why can't Jesus eat raisins?

They keep falling through his hands.

Why couldn't Jesus crucify himself?

He couldn't get the last nail in.

Why did Jesus drown when he tried to walk on water?

Because of the holes in his feet.

What's the difference between Catholics and Universalist Unitarians?

Catholics only make babies; U.U.s fuck.

Vance, a rather uncouth man, went to church one Sunday. He sat down behind a beautiful young woman with a fine round ass. When the time came to rise and sing a hymn, Vance noticed that the woman's skirt was caught between her buttocks. Believing he was doing a good deed, Vance reached out and pulled the skirt free.

Never had such a speech been heard in that church before! In a fierce and furious tongue-lashing, the woman reduced Vance to a tiny mass of quiet, quivering flesh. She then proceeded to move to a different pew. Vance was grateful when the service was over and he could finally leave.

The next Sunday, Vance came to church with his friend Howard. Once again, the same woman was sitting just in front of them. Once again, the time came for them to rise and sing a hymn. Once again, the woman's skirt was caught up her ass. Vance saw his friend Howard reach out and pull the woman's skirt out of her butt. He was mortified. There was only one thing to do. As fast as he could, Vance crammed the skirt right back where it was.

"How dare you do that again," she screamed as she stomped out of the church.

"How typical of women," Vance said to Howard. "They can never make their minds up."

————————

Three proofs that Jesus was Jewish:
　1. He lived at home till he was
　　thirty-three.

2. He went into his father's business.

3. His mother thought he was God.

Three proofs that Jesus was Irish:

1. He never got married.

2. He never held a steady job.

3. His last request was a drink.

Three proofs that Jesus was Puerto Rican:

1. His first name was Jesus.

2. He was always in trouble with the law.

3. His mother didn't know who his father was.

Three proofs that Jesus was Italian:

1. He talked with his hands.

2. He had wine with every meal.

3. He worked in the building trades.

Three proofs that Jesus was from California:

1. He never cut his hair.

2. He walked around barefoot.

3. He invented a new religion.

Three proofs that Jesus was black:

1. He called everybody brother.

2. He had no permanent address.

3. Nobody would hire him.

Reason that the Jews killed Jesus: He refused to become a doctor or lawyer.

————————

One day at a convent, three nuns were having a talk about a particular priest. The first nun said, "I put one of those girlie magazines on his desk, so when he goes in there to work, he'll just have to see it." All the nuns giggled.

The second nun said, "Well, I found out where he keeps his condoms, and the other day I sneaked in and put a tiny pinhole in the tip of each one."

The third nun fainted.

————————

A nun went into a liquor store and asked for a bottle of whiskey. The clerk said, "I'm sorry, Sister, but I can't sell you any alcohol."

"It's for Mother Superior's bowels," she said.

The clerk thought for a moment, then sold her the whiskey.

Later that day, the clerk saw the nun completely shit-faced. He said, "I thought you said that whiskey was for Mother Superior's bowels!"

The nun said, "It is. She's gonna shit when she sees me."

———————

How do you make a nun pregnant?

Fuck her.

Thirteen

Profound Poetry

Raunchy rhymes

Birds do it and fly,
Girls do it and cry,
Dogs do it and stick to it,
So why not you and I?

———————

Ashes to ashes and dust to dust,
If it wasn't for cunts your cock
   would rust.
Sugar is sweet and salt is salt,
If you don't get no nookie it's your
   own damn fault.

———————

The question before us
Is where's her clit-OR-is?

———————

My name is Joe Taylor, my prick is
    a whaler,
My ballocks weigh forty-four pounds,
Where is Miss Hammer? I'll fuck
    her, god damn her,
I'll nail her old ass to the ground.

———————

"A Riddle"

My pretty maid, fain would I know
What thing it is 'twill breed delight;
That strives to stand; that cannot go;
That feeds the mouth that cannot
  bite.
It is the truncheon Mars does use;
A bedward bit that maidens choose.
'Twas neer a maid but by her will
Will keep it in her quiver still.
The fairest maid that eer took life
For love of this became a wife.

———————

Ta-ra-ra boom-der-e
There was no school today.
The teacher passed away;
She died of tooth decay.
She fell into the bay,
The fish all swam away,
And when they took her out
She smelled like sauerkraut.

———————

Hitler has only got one ball;
Goehring's are rather awf'ly small;
Himmler is somewhat sim'lar;
And Goebbels has no balls at all.

———————

I went to the drugstore to get a little
    gin,
But the old son-of-a-bitch wouldn't
    let me in.
So I picked up a rock and I busted
    in the glass,
And out came the devil a-sliding on
    his ass.
Well, the devil shit a monkey and
    the monkey shit a flea,
The flea shit a sailor and the sailor
    went to sea.
Well, the sea began to roar and the
    piss began to pour,
And the sailor got a hard-on so he
    had to come ashore.

———————

"The Night Before Christmas"

'Twas the night before Christmas,
    and all through the house
The whole fucking family was drunk
    and a louse.
With Ma in the whorehouse, and Pa
    smoking grass,
And me settling down to a nice
    piece of ass,
When all of a sudden there arose
    such a clatter
I jumped off my ass to see what's
    the matter.
I looked out the window and saw a
    big dick;
I knew in an instant it must be Saint
    Prick.
He fell down the chimney like a bat
    out of hell;
I knew in an instant the fat fucker fell.
He filled all the stockings with pret-
    zels and beer,
And a big yellow rubber for the fam-
    ily queer.
Then he rose up the chimney and
    flew out of sight,
Saying, "Fuck all of you, and have a
    terrible night!"

There once was an athlete named
 Wong
Who bragged he was hefty and strong,
Because, as a gift,
He would prove he could lift
An object the size of his dong.

———————

There once was a plumber named
 Larry
Whose body was so very hairy
Whenever he'd slouch
Or lean over and crouch,
The sight of his backside was scary.

———————

There once was a poor girl named
 Ann
Who spent all her time on the can.
When she started to cry,
I had to say why:
She just didn't eat enough bran.

———————

There once was a bright girl named
    Kristi
Whose urine was brownish and
    misty.
She would pee in a cup
And then bottle it up
And send it to market as Swiss Tea.

There once was a trucker named
    Scott
Who would fill all the girls with his
    shot.
He would lick 'em and dick 'em
And fuck 'em and prick 'em
But he still couldn't get enough
    twat.

There once was a shepherd named
    Crewes
Whose hard-on he just couldn't lose.
With no girls to assault
Perhaps you can't fault
His putting his dick to good ewes.

———————

"The Fucking Machine"

A sailor told me before he died, I
    don't know whether the bastard
    lied,
He had a wife with a cunt so wide
    she never could be satisfied.
So he invented a fucking wheel, at-
    tached to it a prick of steel,
Two huge balls all filled with cream,
    & ran the whole device with steam.
'Round & 'round went the fucking
    wheel, in & out went the prick of
    steel,
Until, at last, the woman cried,
    "Enough, enough, I'm satisfied."
But now I come to the saddest bit:
    there was no way of stopping it.
The girl was torn from twat to tit,
    and whole fucking thing went up
    in shit.

Fourteen

Condoms

Those friendly sex aids

What's the difference between a coffin and a condom?

They both have stiffs in them, but one's coming and one's going.

———————

Why did the geek put ice in his condom?

To keep the swelling down.

———————

Have you heard about the new designer condom?

It's called Sergio Prevente.

———————

Sign at a company picnic: Have a safe wienie roast—please use a condoment.

———————

Janice: I gave my boyfriend a condom before we had sex.
Gwen: My boyfriend tried a condom once, and he said he'd never use one again.
Janice: Why?
Gwen: He said it was the worst chewing gum he ever tasted.

———————

How does a fag remove a condom?

He farts!

———————

Have you heard about the restaurant that prints your bill on a condom?

That's so you can stick your friend with the check.

———————

Three junkies were sitting around, sharing a needle. Another guy joined them, and they passed him the needle. The guy said, "Are you crazy? Aren't you afraid of getting AIDs?"

"No way, dude," said one of the junkies. "We all got condoms on."

———————

What's the biggest drawback about having safe sex?

Stopping to turn the page.

———————

Why did the pharmacist sell condoms with pinholes in the tips?

Because her husband was getting rich from performing abortions.

———————

What do instant film and a condom have in common?

They both capture that magic moment.

———————

Two kindergartners were talking. One said, "Guess what I found on the veranda last night?"

"What?"

"A condom."

"Cool!" said the second child. "What's a veranda?"

———————

A married woman was having a fling with another man while her husband was at work. In the middle of their activities, the husband came home unexpectedly. The wife's boyfriend, buck naked except for a condom, bolted out an open window and ran down the street.

A jogger saw him puffing by, and called out, "Hey, buddy, how come you're wearin' that rubber?"

"Oh, I usually run totally naked,"the man said, "But today it looked like rain."

A traveling saleswoman was driving through a backwoods area when her car broke down and she had to stay the night at a cabin. The man who lived there told her that she was welcome, but she'd better stay away from his two sons.

Later that night, she went into the first son's room and said, "We can have a little bounce, but you must wear this condom for safety." The son put the condom on, they had passionate sex, and she left his room.

Next, she went to the second son's room. Sneaking in, she told him, "We can have a little bounce, but you must wear this condom for safety." He put the condom on, they had passionate sex, and she went back to her room.

Six months later, the two sons were reading a newspaper when they saw that the traveling saleswoman had just died in a messy car accident. The first son turned to the second son and said, "She's dead. Do you think we can take these condoms off now?"

HAUTALA'S HORROR AND
SUPERNATURAL SUSPENSE

**NOWHERE TO RUN . . . NOWHERE TO HIDE . . .
ZEBRA'S SUSPENSE WILL *GET* YOU—
AND WILL MAKE YOU BEG FOR MORE!**

NOWHERE TO HIDE (4035, $4.50)
by Joan Hall Hovey
After Ellen Morgan's younger sister has been brutally murdered, the
highly respected psychologist appears on the evening news and dares
the killer to come after her. After a flood of leads that go nowhere, it
happens. A note slipped under her windshield states, "YOU'RE IT."
Ellen has woken the hunter from its lair . . . and she is his prey!

SHADOW VENGEANCE (4097, $4.50)
by Wendy Haley
Recently widowed Maris learns that she was adopted. Desperate to
find her birth parents, she places "personals" in all the Texas news-
papers. She receives a horrible response: "You weren't wanted
then, and you aren't wanted now." Not to be daunted, her search
for her birth mother—and her only chance to save her dangerously
ill child—brings her closer and closer to the truth . . . and to
death!

RUN FOR YOUR LIFE (4193, $4.50)
by Ann Brahms
Annik Miller is being stalked by Gibson Spencer, a man she once
loved. When Annik inherits a wilderness cabin in Maine, she finally feels free from his constant threats. But then, a note under
her windshield wiper, and shadowy form, and a horrific nighttime
attack tell Annik that she is still the object of this lovesick madman's obsession . . .

EDGE OF TERROR (4224, $4.50)
by Michael Hammonds
Jessie thought that moving to the peaceful Blue Ridge Mountains
would help her recover from her bitter divorce. But instead of pro-
viding the tranquility she desires, they cast a shadow of terror.
There is a madman out there—and he knows where Jessie lives—
and what she has seen . . .

NOWHERE TO RUN (4132, $4.50)
by Pat Warren
Socialite Carly Weston leads a charmed life. Then her father, a cel-
ebrated prosecutor, is murdered at the hands of a vengeance-seek-
ing killer. Now he is after Carly . . . watching and waiting and
planning. And Carly is running for her life from a crazed murderer
who's become judge, jury—and executioner!

*Available wherever paperbacks are sold, or order direct from the
Publisher. Send cover price plus 50¢ per copy for mailing and
handling to Penguin USA, P.O. Box 999, c/o Dept. 17109,
Bergenfield, NJ 07621. Residents of New York and Tennessee
must include sales tax. DO NOT SEND CASH.*